Outstandi
In A Weel

Gareth Lewis

The Teach Yourself series has been trusted around the world
for over 60 years. This series of 'In A Week' business books is
designed to help people at all levels and around the world to
further their careers. Learn in a week what the experts learn
in a lifetime.

Gareth Lewis (BSc (Hons) PGCE MSc FCIPD) has worked as a consultant in the field of organizational and leadership development for over 25 years. In that time he has worked with many leading companies at senior level to develop products, services and systems. One of his main interests is in applying ideas from psychology to improve performance in organizations. He has written extensively on management issues, and now combines consultancy with his work as a research psychologist.

Outstanding Creativity

Gareth Lewis

www.inaweek.co.uk

Teach® Yourself

Hodder Education

338 Euston Road, London NW1 3BH.

Hodder Education is an Hachette UK company

First published in UK 1999 by Hodder Education

This edition published 2012

Copyright © 1999, 2012 Gareth Lewis

The moral rights of the author have been asserted

Database right Hodder Education (makers)

The *Teach Yourself* name is a registered trademark of Hachette UK.

British Library Cataloguing in Publication Data: a catalogue record for this
title is available from the British Library.

10 9 8 7 6 5 4 3 2 1

The publisher has used its best endeavours to ensure that any website
addresses referred to in this book are correct and active at the time of going
to press. However, the publisher and the author have no responsibility for the
websites and can make no guarantee that a site will remain live or that the
content will remain relevant, decent or appropriate.

The publisher has made every effort to mark as such all words which it
believes to be trademarks. The publisher should also like to make it clear that
the presence of a word in the book, whether marked or unmarked, in no way
affects its legal status as a trademark.

Every reasonable effort has been made by the publisher to trace the copyright
holders of material in this book. Any errors or omissions should be notified
in writing to the publisher, who will endeavour to rectify the situation for any
reprints and future editions.

Hachette UK's policy is to use papers that are natural, renewable and
recyclable products and made from wood grown in sustainable forests.
The logging and manufacturing processes are expected to conform to the
environmental regulations of the country of origin.

www.hoddereducation.co.uk

Typeset by Cenveo Publisher Services.

Printed and bound by CPI Group (UK) Ltd, Croydon, CR0 4YY.

**Also available
in ebook**

Contents

Introduction

Creativity is at the heart of many of the most pressing organizational issues such as change, innovation and knowledge-based products and services. Creative people are desirable assets.

The pace of change only increases. The future poses significant challenges. In order for us to survive and flourish then you, and your organizations, need to develop the skills that will help foster creativity and innovation.

Creativity is not a single notion that can be considered on its own. It is entirely holistic and infiltrates every aspect of an organization. As such, it cannot be ignored.

In this book you will discover ideas and insights into many aspects of creativity. You will explore why creativity is so central to long-term success, and what organizations should be thinking about and doing in order to nurture it.

You will learn about the personal and psychological aspects of creativity, how creative people behave, and how they go about imaginative or original thinking. You will also discover a range of practical problem-solving and creative tools that are easy to learn, easy to remember and easy to put into practice if you are committed to becoming a more creative individual.

This knowledge is vital because, as the world changes, so too we need to change with it. Sometimes we have to follow change, sometimes we may lead it. In both cases, though, there is opportunity to be creative, and to develop personally or improve our organizations.

Creativity isn't about intelligence or formal education. It isn't about how well you may have performed at school or at university. It is about seeing situations and problems with a fresh pair of eyes. About turning threats into opportunities.

About turning weaknesses into strengths. *This book will help you adopt creative approaches to life that protect your own future and that of your organization.*

This week, we will cover:

SUNDAY

The creative imperative

> *As tough and uncertain as the digital world makes it for business, it is evolve or die.*
>
> Bill Gates

Why is creativity important? That is the key question you will address today.

You need to tackle this question to decide whether creativity is a bonus and some kind of luxury or whether there are more fundamental and significant answers.

To do that you will focus on two levels, namely:

- the individual (i.e. you), and
- the organization within the context of the whole economy.

We are going to set out a case that points to the unique combination of factors that make creativity high on the list of priorities for modern businesses and organizations, as well as for you personally.

You will learn about the creative impulse, human curiosity and motivation before we move on to review creativity in an economic and technological context. You will, we hope, agree that our ten predictions about the future form a framework for understanding what is happening to you personally and to any organizations you are involved with. You will conclude today's learning by looking at creativity and innovation as they affect business. The day ends with ten multiple choice questions, as do the rest of the days in the coming week.

The creative impulse

Before we get down to 'business' we should think of creativity in its historical context. We can be tempted into thinking of creativity as a modern invention; however, creativity and innovation have been components of individual and social behaviour since time immemorial. From the very first attempts by people to organize themselves into more effective social groupings, human creativity has played a critical role in the development of society. Human history is a journey punctuated by an almost uncountable series of creative leaps. Spectacular creative leaps include:

- the invention of the wheel
- the cultivation of crops
- the use of tools
- language
- printing
- space travel.

You could surely nominate many of your own.

If we take almost any aspect of human activity we can trace a long line of development that includes the full range of creative human behaviour and ingenuity to solve problems and make developments. For instance, in agriculture, transport, communications, the written word, food preparation, the visual arts, trade and commerce, manufacturing, houses and homes, health and medicine, leisure and entertainment, and so on. Another aspect of our history is that these creative leaps seem to happen at an uneven pace. There have been notable bursts of creative behaviour. Most of us are familiar with many of these:

- the social, political, military and literary achievements of ancient Greece

- the development of sophisticated cultures and civilizations in many areas of the world – the ancient Chinese, for example
- the sheer scale of human creativity applied in the Renaissance to almost all aspects of human life – trade, visual art, architecture, music
- the use of technology to feed the Industrial Revolution.

For each of these you could name a dozen inventions or discoveries that have substantially improved our lot – see if you can.

Curiosity and the quest for evolution

> *Human beings are not the biggest animals. We're not the strongest or fastest. We're not the sharpest in sight or smell. It's amazing how we survived against the fierce creatures of nature. We survived and prospered because of our brains. We evolved to fill the cognitive niche.*
>
> Bill Gates, Business @ the Speed of Thought

The conclusion from all of this is that progress in human and social affairs has always relied on the creative impulses of individuals. Creativity is a component of the way that we tackle living in the world and deal with the problems and challenges that life throws at us.

Our basic psychological make-up has provided us not only with a brain, but with a need to use it. We use it to adapt to our circumstances and environment: to control it. Our curiosity and our ability to use our brains to make sense of the world is what distinguishes us from other species.

When we add the synergy provided by social behaviour, we have the basic conditions for our creative inheritance.

Human motivation

If we move from the historical perspective to look at ourselves, we also see that our approach to the world involves continuous growth and learning. A look at what we know of psychology tells us a number of things:

1 In the first few years of life babies do some remarkable things – they learn to walk and move about; they acquire language; they begin to socialize and make relationships; they develop cognitive skills.
2 Humans are motivated to seek pleasure and satisfaction through physical, intellectual and social means.
3 We retain a need for growth, learning and personal insight (what Maslow called self-actualization) throughout our lives.

What this tells us is that our capacity to learn, to be curious and to seek both to manipulate the world around us and to adapt to it is 'wired' into us from birth. In short, it is impossible for us not to be creative because these are the key elements of creativity.

The emerging world picture

Let us now move our perspective to the wider world around us, and in particular the world of commerce and business, in which most of us work.

Although it is obvious that the twentieth century saw an explosion of creative energy and activity, it is also easy to see that the 21st century is providing changes that are just as dramatic. These changes are visible in a number of areas, but especially in the economy and technology.

The economy

In their book, *Blur: the speed of change in the connected economy*, Stan Davis and Christopher Meyer charted three of the most powerful forces now driving major changes in the economy. They are:

1 Speed: the acceleration of all aspects of business – new product life cycles, time to market, transaction speed.
2 Intangible assets: the economy is being driven by non-physical factors. Prices are based not on materials' costs but on intangible factors such as brands, research, marketing, relationships, etc.
3 Connectivity: links are becoming richer, tighter and faster.

This has the effect of blurring the distinctions between product and service, between organizations and their customers and stakeholders and between management and workforce. There are many examples of this, such as Amazon's website (www.amazon.com). Customers who wish to browse the site for information (and value-added services such as book reviews) are also part of the product (when they contribute a book review).

What distinguishes this new economy from the old is intellectual capital – knowledge, talent and experience. This is where creativity comes in: if the economy is based on knowledge, then brain power defines the critical skill set.

Technology

Technology is certainly rapidly changing the environment in which we live and work. It is said that we are moving into the information age and, along with it, the knowledge economy.
Consider these facts:

● Government statistics show that the percentage of workers in the data services industry is large and growing at a fast pace.
● Two-thirds of US employees work in the services sector.
● Knowledge is becoming our most important product.
● We have seen a substantial growth in internet connections, email and trading and working on or via the internet.

So, as we take these themes and begin to look forward, what do we see?

Ten predictions for the future

1 Globalization – technology conquers distance and organizations can operate anywhere.
2 Technology – communication and information transfer is transforming how we live and work.
3 Social change – we are entering the information age and the knowledge economy. Manufacturing is becoming marginalized.
4 Stakeholder power – organizations are becoming collections of stakeholders.
5 Innovation – as a prerequisite for success.
6 Competitive pressure – the impossibility of resting on your laurels.
7 Diverse workforces – different social mixes (cross-cultural working), expectations (psychological contracts) and working practices (teleworking).
8 Organizational structures – more complex and radical architectures for organizations (e.g. the virtual organization).
9 Lifelong learning – to continually develop our skills, to nurture progress and satisfaction.
10 Speed of change – everything is getting quicker.

The business environment

The pace of invention increases exponentially. You only need to open your eyes and look around to appreciate the overwhelming and massive leaps that have been taken so far this century. On first reading it would seem that businesses and organizations on the whole have responded well to meet the challenges created by social and scientific developments. Try this simple test: list all of the products you encounter today that did not exist 5 years ago, 10 years ago and 50 years ago. And yet, for all the weight of history, and despite the fact that we have experienced significant social, technological and political changes in recent times, it does not necessarily mean that we are well prepared for the future. Business and commerce is not always efficient in its response to the changes around it.

Organizations in the commercial world have not always been well disposed to capitalize on the creativity of the staff that work in them. How many organizations do you know that you would call genuinely creative or innovative? On the whole, organizations are better at stifling creativity than at nurturing it. Although people are clearly naturally creative in the ways that they approach the world around them, this aspect of human behaviour has not always been encouraged or acknowledged by the organizations in which people work.

Most inventions are created within a context and over a period of time. They are rarely accepted at first. There is a process by which they come to fruition. Sometimes that process can unfold in a tortuous and difficult way. We will take just a few examples which will suffice to illustrate the point, even though this was repeated many times over in the last century. In 1938, Chester Carlson invented the xerographic copying process. Carlson's photocopying process initially failed to generate interest – more than 20 companies turned down his idea. 'I was met with an enthusiastic lack of interest', he said later.

Similar stories apply to many of the inventions that we now take for granted, for example:

● wind-up radio
● Post-it note
● Dyson vacuum cleaner.

The stories show how difficult it was for inventors to get organizations to respond, support, promote or commit to their products. And yet, organizations must face the challenges implied by the changes described in the previous section. The message is simple: innovate or die.

Organizations are now seeking to sponsor and encourage creativity in staff, and to change habits and cultures from those ingrained historical ones.

Gary Hamel is a well-known and leading commentator on business strategy and organizational change. He has pointed out that organizations are now more likely to be defined by what they know (core competence) as by what they do. He encourages organizations to focus on the future and on innovation as the primary means of competing, or of surviving even.

Our emerging agenda

At the beginning of this first chapter we posed a question about whether creativity and innovation are desirable or essential. I hope the answer is becoming clearer. Although we can study creativity because it is satisfying and fun, as employees, managers and business leaders we must take the notions of creativity very seriously. The weight of opinion of all those who study and lead changes in our business environment is that we must place innovation at the centre of our thoughts and strategies.

This leaves us with an important set of considerations for the rest of the book:

- Why are creativity and innovation important to my organization?
- Do I know what it means to be creative, and can I develop a language to talk about it?
- Who is creative, and how do they go about it?
- Are the tools and techniques learnable?
- How can they be applied to real organizational problems and situations?
- How can organizations themselves respond?

Summary

Today you will have discovered that our basic argument is twofold.

● First, that creativity is a deeply embedded aspect of the way humans have always acted. People have always been creative – what would be today's equivalent of the invention of the wheel?

● Second, the future we face is one that will require us to be more, not less, creative in our endeavours. Relying on past success is not an option: it is a recipe for disaster on both a personal and a business level.

We have set out some clear, simple and very important messages:

● Creativity and the need to innovate are 'wired' into us at a very basic level – they are features of who we are and how we live in the world. Innovation is one of the things that sets you apart from animals.

● Creativity is not new. We have a spectacular history of creative achievement. Is it likely that there is no longer any need to be creative?

SUNDAY

MONDAY

TUESDAY

WEDNESDAY

THURSDAY

FRIDAY

SATURDAY

- Creative advances in science and technology have provided us with an environment that in itself feeds the creative merry-go-round of business and commercial life. In other words, they create new opportunities for new creativity.

- The world is changing. The ways of living and working that you have become used to are about to change fundamentally and quickly.

- For organizations, the message is clear: innovate or die.

- Organizations have a poor record of nurturing and promoting creativity. This must change.

Fact-check (answers at the back)

1. Which of the following is a good example of the creative impulse?
   a) slavery ❑
   b) discovering how to make pizza ❑
   c) music ❑
   d) parking meters ❑

2. What makes us creative?
   a) physical exercise every morning ❑
   b) speaking more than one language ❑
   c) being curious and using our brains ❑
   d) a vegetarian diet ❑

3. Which of the following best characterizes human motivation?
   a) the strongest people physically are likely to be the most motivated ❑
   b) motivation seems to be wired into us at birth ❑
   c) poor people have poor motivation ❑
   d) only about 10 per cent of the population are motivated at any one time ❑

4. Choose the most important factor for a modern economy:
   a) natural resources such as coal, oil or minerals ❑
   b) intellectual capital ❑
   c) tourism and cultural pursuits ❑
   d) a strong currency ❑

5. One of the following predictions about the future is probably more accurate than the others. Which is it?
   a) we will all have more leisure time ❑
   b) innovation will drive success ❑
   c) sooner or later robots will take over ❑
   d) all politicians will be honest ❑

6. Pick the best innovator in the past decade.
   a) Kodak ❑
   b) Apple ❑
   c) Woolworths ❑
   d) Habitat ❑

7. The most innovative organizations will sell
   a) more of the same products or services to existing customers ❑
   b) the same products or services to new customers ❑
   c) new products or services to new customers ❑
   d) new products or services to existing customers ❑

8. Creativity
   a) is something that has always been part of being human ❑
   b) started just before the Renaissance ❑
   c) started during the Industrial Revolution ❑
   d) started only after the advent of modern computers ❑

9. What will probably be most important in future?
a) taking time to perfect your idea for a great new product or service ❏
b) dominating the local market before tackling the global market ❏
c) undercutting your competitors' prices ❏
d) getting your great new product or service to market quickly ❏

10. Without innovation what is the most likely future for any business?
a) takeover, failure or bankruptcy ❏
b) stability and job security ❏
c) less need to pay for expensive research and development ❏
d) market share will stay constant ❏

SUNDAY

MONDAY

TUESDAY

WEDNESDAY

THURSDAY

FRIDAY

SATURDAY

MONDAY

What is creativity?

> ***[creative attitude] ... first of all requires the***
> ***capacity to be puzzled.***
>
> Erich Fromm

What exactly is creativity? Do you consider yourself to be a creative person? Does your chosen profession enhance or restrict your creative potential? These are important questions that you may, initially, find difficult to answer.

In Sunday's chapter we looked at why creativity is important in business and working life. Today we will move on to consider in more detail what it is that people consider to be creative and how exactly creativity comes about. We will also try to develop a richer description of the issues surrounding the topic.

We can all easily think of creative masterpieces, from the Sistine Chapel to Beethoven's Fifth Symphony. But creativity also surrounds us in everyday life, manifesting itself in many subtle ways, and we will see why you don't need to be called Shakespeare to be considered creative.

As such, we shall take a look at the various definitions of creativity, and we will see that there is no one simple dictionary definition. Then we shall briefly examine the issues raised by this complexity. Finally, we shall look at the stages of the creative process, and consider if creativity in the domain of, for example, accountancy is just as relevant as it is in the domain of visual art.

By the end of the chapter, you will have a much better idea of how to answer these initial questions.

The shock of the new

We all think that we know what is creative. Most of us, if asked to identify creative people from the past or present, would have little trouble in naming many of the more obvious names, even if we might want to debate the relative merits of each in turn. For example, Leonardo da Vinci, Wolfgang Amadeus Mozart, Albert Einstein and Steven Spielberg.

It is an interesting game to play to consider what are the greatest inventions and creative works of human achievement. This particular point in history is a good time to take stock. What would be your own top ten? In a magazine survey, a list of the top 100 inventions was compiled from the votes of readers and the recommendations of a team of experts. The top five were:

1 Sanitation: after 20,000 Londoners died in a cholera epidemic in 1850 it was decided something should be done. Cities all over Europe followed suit.
2 The computer: the idea was invented by the British mathematician Charles Babbage in the nineteenth century, but the electronic computer was not available for commercial use until after the Second World War.
3 The printing press: invented in 1450 by Johannes Gutenberg. After this, knowledge became available to all.
4 Fire: first used systematically from about 9,000 years ago. What would we do without it?
5 The wheel: presumably derived from rolling logs to move stones possibly about 5,500 years ago.

Others that made the top 100 include the radio (6th), antibiotics (7th), the internet (8th), the transistor (9th), the laser (10th), contraception (12th), plastic (14th), flight (15th), the electric light (18th), the car (23rd), maps (28th), money (29th), the telephone (34th) and photography (38th).

Even in the fields of scientific and technological innovation, the twentieth century did not dominate.

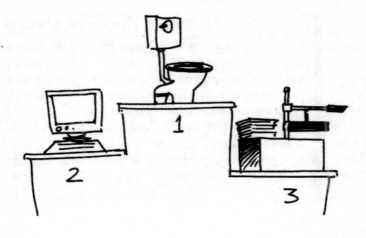

By way of contrast, what are the great and lasting creative masterpieces of history? Some time ago, *The Sunday Times* asked this question to its readers. The top five make interesting reading:

1 *Hamlet* by William Shakespeare
2 'David' by Michelangelo
3 'Pieta' by Michelangelo
4 *King Lear* by William Shakespeare
5 The Sistine Chapel by Michelangelo.

The top 50 were shared between books and plays, art and sculpture, music, buildings and one film. Interestingly enough, science and mathematics were represented only by one book – Charles Darwin's *On the Origin of Species*. Very few works of the twentieth century made it to the list (The Beatles, *Citizen Kane*, James Joyce's *Ulysses* and Sydney Opera House being among the exceptions).

But creativity does not just reside in a limited number of great works or world-changing inventions. It exists in every area of human activity. There are a multitude of everyday manifestations of what we would generally agree to be creative.

The nature of creativity

Creativity touches many aspects of our thinking, social and
acting lives. In this chapter there is a map of the territory,
showing some of the important associated concepts.

Even if we focus just on the generation of novel or inventive
phenomena, we use a variety of words to describe that aspect
of creativity; for instance, produce, create, originate, invent,
discover, conceive, imagine, form, construct, think up, ideate,
devise, originate or envisage.

This in itself suggests that the single word 'creativity' describes
a complex and multifaceted set of phenomena. Some terms have
overlapping meanings and need to be considered separately:

- Creativity is producing or bringing something into existence.
- Creativity, in relation to a person, is a talent for imaginative
  creation.
- Innovation is the introduction of new things or methods.
- Discovery is finding or realizing something not known before.

This suggests that there are different ways to be creative, and
there are different criteria by which to judge creative outcomes.

For a word that is in such everyday use, there is remarkably
little agreement on what exactly it is, especially as we can
see creativity and the results of creative acts all around us.
It is precisely because of this diversity of human activity and

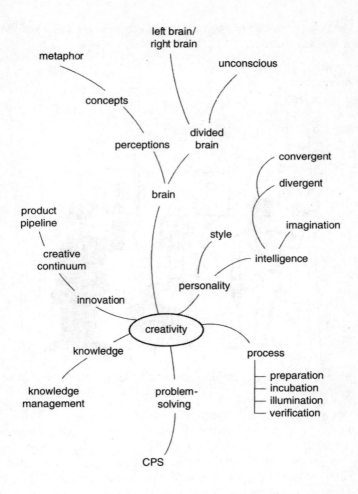

products that it is difficult to tie the word down to a single notion on which we can all agree. It is not only the people and products on which we differ, but the whole notion of what we consider creativity to be.

Creativity (as opposed to individual creative output, such as works of art) has only really been studied in any depth in the last half a century or so. It is therefore fair to say that our ideas on creativity are still only being formed.

What we consider to be creative is certainly related to some of these attributes:

- newness or novelty
- originality
- uniqueness
- the 'eureka' effect
- the out of the ordinary or atypical
- cleverness.

Here are some of the varying definitions for creativity that have been offered:

- 'Mental processes that lead to solutions, ideas, conceptualisations, artistic forms, theories or products that are unique or novel.' (Penguin's *Dictionary of Psychology*)
- 'Any process by which something new is produced – an idea or an object, including a new form or arrangement of old elements.' (Harmon, *Social and technological determiners of creativity*, 1955)
- The process of sensing difficulties, problems, gaps in information, missing elements, something askew; making guesses and formulating hypotheses about these deficiencies; evaluating and testing these guesses and hypotheses; possibly revising and retesting them; and finally communicating the results.' (Torrance, *The nature of creativity as manifest in its testing*, 1988)

Notice that this last one is a fairly detailed description of a process or sequence of steps.

The creative process

In all the research on creativity, there are between 50 and 60 definitions of the word. They differ in their emphasis on three aspects of the total process:

1 An individual: there is a person (or in some cases, as we shall discuss later, a group). Their inputs are the thinking skills and the associated ideas that they bring.
2 A process: these thinking skills are applied through time, in various stages of a sequence.
3 The product or outcome: this is often also in the form of an idea, model, theory or plan (in which case the whole process starts again). It can also be in the form of a tangible result such as a written document, a piece of music, a product, and so on.

The creative individual

As we have already said, it is not too difficult to come up with a list of well-known figures, current or historical, who most would agree were creative. But it does beg some interesting questions:

● Is a person more creative if they write poems in their spare time rather than play football?
● Are novelists more creative than accountants?
● Would you call your child's first finger painting creative? (Many proud parents, of course, would.)
● Are we all creative or should the term creative be the preserve of only a special few?

There is clearly something special about those whose creative efforts change the world or the way that we think about it. This is sometimes referred to as Creativity with a capital 'C'. However, although there is some disagreement on this, it would be too pessimistic to confine the term creativity to this handful of special individuals throughout history. On the other hand:

- Is creativity brilliant conversation? No.
- Is creativity experiencing the world in novel ways? No.

Creativity occurs when the product has been judged to have some value. This implies, though, that the product or output has to be evaluated. How is this done, and by whom? We will explore these ideas below. There are also two further questions, which are important enough for us to consider separately on Wednesday: are the people who we consider creative different, and how do they do things differently?

Creative products

All the questions above imply that to accept an outcome or product as creative other considerations must be involved. Mihaly Csikszentmihalyi has proposed that creativity is in the interrelations between these considerations. Therefore, creativity is a property of a system which is made up of three parts:

1 The domain: this is a set of symbolic rules and procedures which make up a body of knowledge. Science, mathematics and visual art are all domains. Each can be broken down into

finer-grained domains. For our purposes we can also think of examples of more relevant domains:
- management
- accountancy
- mobile communications
- book publishing
- retail
- information services.

2 The person: who can apply and transform the body of knowledge into new ideas or patterns.

3 The field: the set of individuals who act as gatekeepers or judges of new ideas. They are the ones who select ideas and products for recognition. Acceptance can come in many forms:
- management (accepting business propositions)
- customers (who buy or don't buy)
- peers or colleagues
- journals or trade associations (e.g. the Oscars for cinema).

It is worth saying, of course, that creativity may be only one of a number of criteria that any of these bodies apply to new ideas or propositions.

This brings us full circle, because it enables us now to answer the question about what is creative and what is not. The simple answer is that things are creative when they are judged to be creative by the field in question. It gets us out of the dilemma that anything we think is creative must, indeed, be so. It also means that we do not have to be Shakespeare or Michelangelo to be creative. If our domain of choice is paper-folding, we can be creative there if we produce something that is seen as valuable and creative within that fraternity. We don't need an all-purpose set of criteria to apply to any product, as each set of judges (the field) will have a level of agreement as to what constitutes genuine novelty and creativity.

Furthermore, in most domains, there is a natural and continuous process of evolution. This means that ideas, models, theories and products are always changing. They develop new characteristics as people contribute new perspectives and ways of thinking.

Summary

We have learned today that creativity is a complex subject: there is a huge range of things that we call creative and a massive vocabulary to call on, and there is no one agreed definition.

Creativity is not restricted to a limited number of great works or world-changing inventions. We are surrounded by creativity every day, even – especially – in the workplace. Furthermore, creativity exists in all fields of business: from accountancy to footballing to information technology.

We have learnt that our ideas and theories on creativity are still forming and evolving. It has generally been agreed, though, that there is a particular sequence of events leading to the creative outcome, involving the individual, the process and the product or outcome – although researchers differ on their emphasis on each of these three aspects.

SUNDAY

MONDAY

TUESDAY

WEDNESDAY

THURSDAY

FRIDAY

SATURDAY

Creative products are themselves a system involving three elements: the individual, the domain and the field. This is how things are judged to be creative. So, for example, it is up to the American Academy of Motion Picture Arts and Sciences (*field*) to judge whether a particular actor (*individual*) has been genuinely novel and creative in his or her latest film (*domain*) – and award him or her an Oscar in recognition of this.

Fact-check (answers at the back)

1. The top five inventions, according to *Focus* magazine, are:
a) computer, DVD player, television, telephone, camera ❏
b) sanitation, computer, printing press, fire, the wheel ❏
c) MP3 player, washing machine, penicillin, aeroplane, contraception ❏
d) light bulb, computer, camera, telephone, television ❏

2. Only two persons' work feature in *The Sunday Times'* list of top five creative masterpieces. They are:
a) Michelangelo and Shakespeare ❏
b) John Lennon and Shakespeare ❏
c) Jane Austen and Alfred Hitchcock ❏
d) Leonardo da Vinci and John Lennon ❏

3. Creativity manifests itself...
a) every day ❏
b) every other day ❏
c) once a year ❏
d) every couple of months ❏

4. Which statement is true?
a) There is a standard definition of creativity on which everyone in the world has agreed. ❏
b) There is only way to be creative and only one criterion by which creativity is judged. ❏
c) There are different ways to be creative and there are different criteria by which to judge creative outcomes. ❏
d) Our ideas on creativity have already been formally defined and are not evolving. ❏

5. There are three aspects to creativity. These are:
a) the individual, the process, the product or outcome ❏
b) the individual, the parents, the children ❏
c) place of birth, age, sex ❏
d) diet, age, product ❏

6. Creativity with a capital 'C' is...
a) poor creativity ❏
b) creativity that changes the world ❏
c) pretend creativity ❏
d) crazy creativity ❏

7. Which statement is correct?
a) Creativity occurs when the product has been judged to have some value. ❏
b) The term creativity should be restricted to a handful of special individuals throughout history. ❏
c) A footballer is more creative than an accountant. ❏
d) We have to be as good as Michelangelo to be considered creative. ❏

8. Something is considered creative when . . .
a) It sells more than a million copies. ❏
b) It is liked by critics but not the general public. ❏
c) It is judged to be creative by the field in question. ❏
d) It has become a household name. ❏

9. Creative products are a system involving three elements. These are:
a) individual, location, attitude ❏
b) place of birth, field, age ❏
c) age, diet, domain ❏
d) individual, domain, field ❏

10. Which statement is true?
a) It is easy to fake creativity. ❏
b) Creativity is not a complex subject. ❏
c) Paper-folding is creative. ❏
d) One can go from being not creative to creative within a day. ❏

SUNDAY

MONDAY

TUESDAY

WEDNESDAY

THURSDAY

FRIDAY

SATURDAY

TUESDAY

The creative computer

Let us learn to dream and perhaps we will discover the truth.

Kekule

The brain is the factory where our ideas and imagination are formed, so today we will take some time to focus on it in detail. Most of this week we shall be considering how we use our conscious brain to inform ideas and actions in the world. Today we shall consider not only the conscious but the unconscious brain, and explore the important relationship between the two. We will review some of the basic facts about the brain, which can help us to understand the way that creativity operates. We shall also learn about the physical properties of the brain and how these relate to conscious cognitive processing. The main focus of the chapter will be the cerebral cortex, which is responsible for higher-level brain functioning.

Although we shall learn about divisions within the brain, such as between the left and right hemispheres, the outcome for today is to understand the brain not as divided, but as a holistic entity, where each part is complementary to the overall functioning of the whole. This will allow us to understand the way in which creativity takes place holistically, across the brain.

Inside the brain

The brain is an incredible instrument. It is mind-boggling in its complexity. It is the processor at the centre of the nervous system. All of the information received from the outside world is processed here, and it generates the signals for all of the other organs and structures in the body to act.

The brain itself is broken down into a number of distinct physical components, some of which are quite primitive and operate the body's systems, outside of our conscious control. The component that we will look at is the cerebral cortex, at the front and top of the brain, which is responsible for many of the higher functions of the brain such as language, thought, processing of sound and so on.

The basic building blocks of the different components are neurons. It is estimated that there are about 10 billion neurons in the cerebal cortex, and that each can have many millions of connections with other neurons. As a neuron can 'fire' up to 500 hundred times a second, an awesome amount of processing power is made.

In the cerebral cortex, these neurons are collected into groupings that relate to the different functions of the brain. Some of these functions are quite localized. For instance, some kinds of visual processing take place in an identifiable location in the brain. However, other functions, such as memory, can be widely distributed throughout the brain, in the cerebal cortex and elsewhere too.

So the physical components of the brain relate to each other and to our conscious cognitive processing in complex and non-linear ways that are difficult to model. This is typical of any complex adaptive system. But it is possibly the most impenetrable that there is. It also poses some questions that are really in the realm of metaphysics – such as the relationship between the brain and the mind, where consciousness comes from, and so on. Such massive complexity makes it difficult to understand in detail how the brain works. In fact, there is almost certainly more that we don't know about the brain than we do know.

It also explains why people over the years have cast around for an appropriate metaphor to assist in our understanding of the brain. Is it a machine? No, it's too complicated for that. Is it a computer? This is nearer the mark, as the brain can be understood as a sophisticated data-processing device. However, there are also severe limitations even to this metaphor, as there are many ways in which it does not resemble a computer. This word of caution is necessary, as a metaphor is just that – it is a device that helps us to grasp just some of the complexity by making it simple.

The divided brain

Much effort has been devoted by psychologists and neurologists to understand this modular structure and function of the brain. By using equipment that records the electrical activity of the brain, scientists can relate what is happening in the mind to the activity within the brain. Psychologists study phenomena such as perception and memory.

Split brain theory

About 30 years ago, Sperry, Gazzaniga and colleagues studied a group of people who had already had the connection (the corpus callosum) that divides the two halves of the brain severed. They observed what happened when the two hemispheres of the brain were unable to communicate. They discovered that these two halves seem to perform different but complementary functions. This idea has been much quoted and much used in books on creativity. In the original formulation, the different halves of the brain were said to work in the following ways:

Left brain

- analytical
- logical
- verbal (the site of language)
- numerical
- sequential.

It was seen as being the more conscious, logical brain that controlled our rational processes.

Right brain

- holistic
- pattern-forming
- emotional
- spatial
- musical.

It was seen to be the seat of holistic, playful imagination, characterized by ambiguity and metaphor.

LEFT   RIGHT

Thus, the argument went that true creativity involved engaging the right brain, which we were deemed to use very little of in our normal working environment. If only we could be more 'right brained', then creativity would surely flow. This was a seductive argument, followed by many commentators.

Unfortunately, research since the 1970s has somewhat clouded the picture. The emerging reality seems much more complicated than before, and even the principal commentators seem to disagree as to the precise functions of the different halves of the brain.

Whatever the merits of the competing arguments, it seems sensible to accept that there are a large number of sophisticated data-processing and concept-forming functions distributed within the brain, and that creative acts almost certainly involve many or all of them at various stages.

Perhaps we should worry less about the detailed arguments of the academics and accept the split-brain theory as a useful metaphor in its own right that serves to remind us of different 'modes' of thought processing that contribute to the creative process.

Also, we shouldn't lose sight of the fact that many sophisticated thought processes need both sides of the brain in order to be fulfilled. Understanding jokes is a good case in point, for instance, as it requires you to process information both literally and intuitively.

From visible brain to invisible brain

A distinction that is perhaps just as useful as the left/right brain distinction is the one between the conscious or 'visible' part of the brain and the less conscious or completely unconscious part of the brain.

left brain/right brain

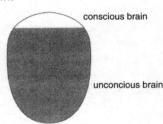

conscious brain

unconcious brain

It is fairly easy to demonstrate that:

1 very strange things happen 'down there', below the level of consciousness, and
2 what happens under (and/or just at the surface) of consciousness is vital in many aspects of creative thinking.

39

Let us illustrate point 1.

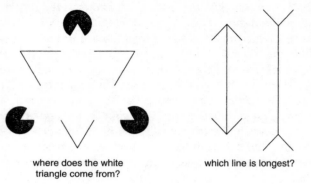

where does the white triangle come from?

which line is longest?

These optical illusions clearly show that some strange things happen to our perceptions out of our conscious control, and that the reality that the mind produces often bears only a passing resemblance to the reality 'out there'.

It also demonstrates the tenuous relationship between conscious and unconscious processing. However, as we shall see later, this can be used to our advantage.

Higher functions

Creativity is associated with many of the higher-level functions of the brain. The spider diagram in the 'Monday' chapter illustrates some of the more important ones. (The relationships illustrated there are entirely personal, and you are invited to re-map them for yourself.)

We will select just two of these to examine their relationship to creative thinking.

Concepts

Concepts are one of the keys to our higher cognitive functioning. They are part of our way of understanding and processing the huge amounts of perceptual information and making it digestible and operable. Our ability to conceptualize is one of the major distinctions between us and other life forms.

But how do concepts come about? They come about through our ability to generalize our experience and sort our thoughts into categories. It should go without saying that we form categories or concepts in highly individualized ways. In itself, it is a function of our creativity that we can do this. The ability to form and re-form information into categories gives us an ever-sensitive hold on the world around us.

There is a school of thought: the mathematician Douglas R Hofstadter (who can be considered a school of thought in his own right) proposed that much of our ability to be creative comes from what he calls the 'slippability' of these categories.

Slippability refers to the ability of our concepts or categories to overlap and move from one into another. It might be reasoned that if our ability to make concepts is important then the stronger or more solidly we do this the better – with each concept clearly separated from all others. However, all concepts do have an element of 'fuzziness' at the border. When concepts overlap and merge into each other (to some degree) this can lead to a creative fusion.

concepts don't overlap –
rigid thinking

concepts overlap –
creative thinking

This can happen quite easily in normal circumstances, although on the whole such overlap of concepts tends to happen accidentally and unconsciously. Malapropisms and Freudian slips are good examples of this accidental creative fusion. For skilled thinkers, the overlap of concepts can also be engineered to some extent to produce variations on concepts and hybrid concepts, and thus totally new ways of seeing the world.

This overlap of categories is a kind of 'twiddling of the knobs' or a making of variations on a theme. It can provide a good explanation for the generation of creative ideas. It might be argued that such 'twiddling' or making variations on a theme is trivial when compared with the titanic ideas we associate with the giants of creativity. Yet these great thinkers on the whole do not think in an entirely different way from us ordinary mortals.

The history of great inventions and great works shows that they are all based very solidly on ideas and themes laid down by their predecessors and contemporaries. What they have done is to re-interpret them and re-present them, and thus change the way we see or perceive the world.

Making variations on a theme is the crux of creativity

The role of intuition

Much of our ability to process and make sense of the data, perceptions, concepts and so on, under the level of consciousness, is called intuition. (It is an interesting aside that a word we all know, used throughout history, only recently has come to have a scientific basis.)

> ### *Intuition is evolution's default strategy for solving problems.*
> Steven Pinker

There are different versions of the world represented by the division between the conscious and the unconscious. The brain soaks up information and makes patterns and connections all the time without your noticing. The result is a body of knowledge of which you are not aware. It can't be verbalized, because verbalization is in the more conscious aspects of the brain. However, information lost to conscious recall can still influence behaviour and decisions.

Furthermore, it seems that we can also learn and recall without being consciously aware of it. It is called implicit learning. As a result of this, people can understand connections and rules that they can neither recall nor verbalize.

This suggests that a good strategy for learning or problem-solving is to put the information and influences in and let the brain do the work. Can it be that simple? Gary Klein, an Ohio-based consultant psychologist, has looked at how professionals deal with situations when time is short, the stakes are high and there is incomplete information. What he has found is that experienced professionals often bypass the more thoughtful, logical and rational decision-making processes. This is fine, of course, as long as the decisions based on intuition are as good or better than those arrived at by more methodical means.

Klein devised experiments in which some subjects were asked to take their time and think before making a decision and others were asked for a snap decision. He found that the 'thoughtful' subjects were more likely to change their minds. So what does this tell us? It suggests that:

1 In some circumstances, intuition will serve us very well as it harnesses the unconscious processing power of the brain.
2 The brain has an 'implicit' memory and processing system working away out of sight, and there is growing evidence to support this.

In fact, this also makes 'common' sense. A snap decision or an immediate intuitive decision is one where you are using your intuition to access the knowledge that has been stored in your brain quietly over time. The British mathematician and philosopher George Spencer Brown summed it up when he said that to arrive at even a simple truth you need years of contemplation, '...not activity. Not reasoning. Not calculating. Not busy behaviour of any kind.'

How often have you heard the phrase 'sleep on it'? We have always valued the invisible processes that are involved in reflection and contemplation.

Yet in modern organizations we are too 'left brained' – too rational and logical. This leaves little time for altered states and playful approaches that give the associative and intuitive brain time to build the connections that it needs.

Summary

Today we have wandered into the territory of knowledge about the brain to explore the way that the brain functions and how this is important for creative thinking. We have learnt about the complexity of the brain and how our understanding of it has changed and developed through time. Our insight into the brain can allow us to draw out some useful points in relation to creative thinking:

● We can distinguish between the right and left hemispheres of the brain. It was originally thought that creativity involved engaging the right side of the brain; however, since the 1970s it has become accepted that creative acts require many or all of the functions of the brain, involving both the left and right hemispheres.

● Creativity is associated with higher-level brain functions, which are distributed across the brain.

● Our ability to create concepts, or to sort our thoughts into categories, is a function of our creativity.

- Our ability to be creative comes largely from the 'slippability' of concepts. This overlapping of categories provides us with new ways of seeing the world.
- Creative thinking involves both the conscious and unconscious mind. Intuition, a body of knowledge of which you are not aware, exists in the unconscious and is greatly involved in creative thinking and decision-making.

Fact-check (answers at the back)

1. What are the basic building blocks of the brain?
   a) protons ❑
   b) neutrons ❑
   c) electrons ❑
   d) neurons ❑

2. What is the cerebral cortex responsible for?
   a) the operation of the body's system outside of our conscious control ❑
   b) higher functions of the brain such as language and thought processing ❑
   c) bodily movements ❑
   d) the nervous system ❑

3. What is split brain theory?
   a) the theory that the brain is divided into lots of complementary parts ❑
   b) the theory that the brain is split between the conscious and unconscious parts ❑
   c) the theory that the left and right hemispheres of the brain perform different but complementary functions ❑
   d) the theory that the left and right hemispheres of the brain are distinct and operate completely independently of one another ❑

4. The right side of the brain was said to be:
   a) logical ❑
   b) numerical ❑
   c) analytical ❑
   d) emotional ❑

5. To be truly creative what must we engage?
   a) both sides of our brain ❑
   b) the left side of our brain ❑
   c) the right side of our brain ❑
   d) only the conscious part of our brain ❑

6. What does slippability refer to?
   a) the ability of concepts to change ❑
   b) the movement of concepts within the brain ❑
   c) the overlapping and merging of concepts ❑
   d) the way that concepts collide with one another ❑

7. Creative fusion happens when:
   a) concepts collide ❑
   b) concepts are clearly defined ❑
   c) concepts overlap and merge ❑
   d) a new concept is made ❑

8. When professionals are forced to make snap decisions they:
   a) tend to make the wrong decision ❑
   b) make decisions based on intuition ❑
   c) make decisions using the right side of the brain ❑
   d) change their minds about the decision made ❑

9. When we have a lot of time to make a decision we:
   a) tend to make the right decision ❏
   b) tend to make the wrong decision ❏
   c) feel satisfied with the decision made ❏
   d) change our minds about the decision made ❏

10. In organizations, when decision-making we tend to:
    a) make rational or logical decisions ❏
    b) make intuitive decisions ❏
    c) make decisions using the right side of our brain ❏
    d) allow the use of our unconscious to guide decisions ❏

WEDNESDAY

Being creative

Originality is simply a fresh pair of eyes.

Woodrow Wilson

Today we shall look at creative people and examine what it is that makes a person creative. What are the processes that are involved in creative imagination? Are creative people different from others? If so, how are they different?

We shall use examples of famous 'creative people' to allow us to come up with some generalizations about what it is that defines a creative person. We will look at how intelligence is a factor in successful creativity, but how it is not necessarily a 'given', and how creativity can be acquired or built upon over a lifetime. We will also look at the specific personality traits of creative people: their wide range of behaviours and fluidity in moving from one behavioural extreme to another. While it might be assumed that, like intelligence, personality traits are a natural given, we will learn how we can practise new skills and strategies to improve our capacity for creative behaviour.

It is intended that by understanding more about creative people and creative processes we can learn how to use these ideas to improve our creative output. Creativity can be enhanced and achieved not by accident, but by following specific steps to success.

Creative people

Following on from the arguments in Monday's chapter, we should be clear that when we talk of creative people, we are not confining ourselves to people who just:

- have unusual ideas
- are interesting or stimulating
- see the world in novel ways
- do or say bizarre or 'off-the-wall' things.

Rather, we are talking about people who make a significant and recognized contribution within their own field.

Life history

One way of delving into the personal nature of creativity is to study the lives and personalities of the geniuses of history. There have been many studies of the lives of accepted giants from the world of science, music, literature and the arts. We will look at what we know about their personalities from such studies. But, first of all, it is worth noting that the lives of many of these people do seem to involve a higher incidence of certain features than the lives of the rest of us. Here are some common features:

- significant loss (particularly of parents) at a young age
- family disruption and dysfunction
- incredibly productive; for example, Picasso produced over 20,000 works, Edison produced 1,093 patents and Freud produced 330 publications
- not afraid to ask child-like questions, such as Albert Einstein's 'What would happen if I could ride on a ray of light?', which allegedly led him to the special theory of relativity
- intense period of immersion in the domain before major breakthroughs are made
- 'fruitful asynchrony' or being different from the pack.

Intelligence

Intelligence was first put forward as a means of predicting educational and life achievement. It was measured in the form of intelligence quotient (IQ). This has turned out to be a difficult concept that has fallen somewhat into disrepute. These days we use the term 'fluid intelligence' to describe a range of cognitive skills important in the more analytical aspects of problem-solving and creativity.

It does seem to be that, on the whole, creative people are more intelligent than the general population. However, the reverse is not also true. That is, being intelligent does not guarantee being creative. It seems to be that to be creative, you need 'just enough' fluid intelligence.

The 'sister' concept to fluid intelligence is crystallized intelligence, which is that born of skills and knowledge about the world. You acquire and deepen this over a lifetime. Previously, we have suggested that knowledge and understanding of a domain is an important factor in creative achievement. This correlates with the idea that crystallized intelligence is an important factor in creativity.

Howard Gardner, in his book *Frames of Mind*, put forward the idea that we have a range of intelligences and that we each use different aspects of our creative potential to a different degree. The aspects of intelligence are:

- visuospatial
- verbal
- personal
- musical
- logico-mathematical
- bodily.

Daniel Goleman says that one of the intelligences is emotional intelligence. Certainly, this notion is gathering momentum and support, and it would be a good indicator of creativity in social and interpersonal or behavioural contexts.

Personality traits

Creative people come in all shapes and sizes, and that applies to character and personal preferences as well as physical attributes. There are very few traits that seem to apply to all creative people. Are they more extrovert? It seems they are both more and less. Are they more competitive or co-operative? In fact they seem to be both. This is the contradiction. One thing that seems to set creative people aside is their cognitive complexity. On many of the important scales of measuring or describing human behaviour they seem to be able to move and adapt fluidly from one extreme to the other with more facility than other people. In short, they have contradictory extremes.

Here are descriptions of some of the more interesting contradictions, as set out by Mihaly Csikszentmihalyi in *Flow and the Psychology of Discovery and Invention*.

1 Energy: they manage to control their own energy levels, being both energetic and restful and reflective at appropriate moments.
2 Intelligence: they have sufficient intelligence, together with an ability to pose naive, child-like questions. Certainly creative people tend to have a fluency and flexibility of thought.
3 Discipline: controlled discipline means that highly creative people can move from disciplined perseverance and hard work to playfulness and distance.
4 Fantasy and imagination: again, they are able to move fluently between flights of imagination and rooted reality. Reality can be coped with if it moves and shifts.
5 Introversion versus extroversion: they are able to move from being the social isolate to the centre of attention. They have the ability to stand their own company yet be comfortable in the company of others.
6 Humility versus pride: they can express the range from arrogance to self-deprecation. This is related to aggressive/ambitious versus selfless/altruistic.
7 Masculine versus feminine: they are able to express both aspects of their sexuality.
8 Independence/rebellion versus tradition/conservativeness.
9 Passion versus objectivity: people can evaluate situations with both the head and the heart.
10 Openness versus sensitivity: they are able to look both outward and inward, which means extremes of emotion – pain and pleasure/enjoyment.

Like all such lists, no one person will be able to express the full range of each of these scales. The argument is that creative people are more likely to have a fuller repertoire of behaviour than is average.

Other studies, more grounded in creative behaviour in the working environment, suggest that those considered creative tend to be more:

- tolerant of uncertainty and ambiguity
- self-confident
- unconventional
- original in thought and deed
- intrinsically motivated
- intelligent
- determined to succeed.

Enhancing creativity

How do people apply their skills and preferences in the creative process? As long ago as 1926, Graham Wallas, in *The Art of Thought*, based on his account of eminent creators, proposed a four-stage model of creative thinking:

1 Preparation: focus on the task and collection of relevant information.
2 Incubation: a transfer to unconscious or involuntary work.
3 Illumination: when the essence of the problem emerges in a 'eureka' moment.
4 Verification: more conscious rational processes used to evaluate the insight.

It is interesting how consistent this is with our views about the importance of intuition and unconscious or 'invisible' processing.

It should not be assumed that these are four sequential stages that must be followed through to achieve success. Rather they show that insight is achieved not by accident but by a combination of processes that include:

- sorting the wood from the trees – immersing ourselves in information, and selecting appropriately

- fitting the pieces of the jigsaw together – fluidly combining and connecting ideas and concepts, often unconsciously
- reality checking – evaluating insights against real-world criteria.

On the basis of understanding more about creative people and creative processes, we need to ask how we can use these ideas to help us improve our creative output.

Individual creativity

The discussion above focuses primarily on what people are – their preferences and characteristics. For a moment, we should also think about how they apply both their talents and the approaches discussed. We are what we are and there are some basic aspects of our personality that we cannot change. However, we can practise new skills and we can enhance our repertoire. It seems that there are four things, above all, needed to be a creative thinker:

1 A tremendous amount of information – memory sharpened by practice and positive feedback.
2 A willingness to generate ideas – for fun and enjoyment.
3 A large waste bin – you must be willing to evaluate and to discriminate between the junk and the good ideas.
4 A surplus of energy and attention – you must be willing to devote all your spare energy to your own area of interest.

JUNK   INFO   IDEA GENERATOR

Strategies for improving creativity

- Use all of your brain.
- Access the unconscious.
- Reinstate the intuitive.

- Loosen your concepts – use fluidity.
- Develop a sense of curiosity – ask challenging questions.
- Do things you enjoy – and enjoy things you do.
- Immerse yourself in what you are good at.

There is one final piece of advice that all good creative practitioners have recourse to, and that relates to when and where they are most creative.

Creating the right environment

Archimedes did it in the bath. Newton found it under the apple tree. Where are you most creative? We can take a lead from others who are considered creative achievers.

Jean Lammiman and Michael Syrett of Roffey Park Management Institute, in *Innovation at the Top*, studied how and when senior managers and directors were creative.

They report that one senior manager finds inspiration in surprising ways, some of which include the way that different essences make a perfume; the way a chef prepares food – care, attention to detail and quality; Zen philosophy; and the harmony of music. He says: 'Music is the language which uses creative processes rather than words.'

The perspective of senior managers is shaped by what they read, watch, listen to and experience in private. It is clear from the study that interests outside the workplace influence decision-making. The majority of the best ideas occurred away from the workplace in natural settings such as during train or plane journeys or while walking, relaxing or playing music. Sport and comedy seem to be featured highly. Here are some of the most mentioned stimuli:

- humour and wit on radio and television
- networking
- talking to passengers on a train
- conversation or contact with colleagues
- 'dreaming and drifting' (this often happens in the oddest places: gardening, opera, etc., but can result in breakthrough ideas)
- the community and specialist groups for stimulus and support
- reading – some find inspiration through a fictional character or historical personality
- radio – stimulates the imagination in a particular way
- leisure – renews skills and enthusiasm
- time alone for creative thought.

All achievers are creative in their own particular way. A self-taught chef finds inspiration and wild herbs while running in his native hills in the southern Auvergne. Michael Bras, who achieved a third Michelin star in 1999, learnt cookery from his mother. His specialism is wild and unusual plants, and he says: 'I run several times a week in the mountains and it is from these runs that I harvest ideas and emotions.' He finds his inspiration in nature, and hopes to express through his food 'a climate, a freedom of expression, a sense of wonderment, a joie de vivre'. He compares his cooking to jazz, 'for its architecture ... its fluid elegance, its silences'.

> Source: 'Michelin honours poetic chef of Auvergne',
> *Independent*, 2 March 1999

'to sleep, perchance to dream'

There is a wealth of research that shows that sleep can have a positive influence on human performance, and creativity is a component of that.

A good night's sleep can make you 40% smarter.

Harvard Medical School

Sleep is also crucial to memory formation and learning. That is, sleep is not passive – it is active in the functioning of the brain. In particular, REM (rapid eye movement) sleep relates to the cortex of the brain. This is the storehouse of associative memory. It is good at processing context – just like certain aspects of creativity. Good sleep allows us to process facts and perceptions and build them into coherent patterns.

The sleeping brain has been called the 'creative worry factory'. It relies on imagery, metaphor and symbolism. The combination of hard logical working thoughts and the lateral thinking, dreaming brain enhances creativity. There are many examples of this kind of creative dreaming from the respected achievers of history.

The problem is that in our modern society we are often too busy to get the right amount of sleep. If we are right about the critical role of the unconscious in creative thought, then the role of sleep and deep relaxation may need to be re-evaluated.

Summary

Today we have concentrated on perhaps the most important consideration of all: the personality and functions of the individual brain. We have learnt that creative people are often:

- used to adverse or unusual life experiences
- extremely productive
- intelligent
- cognitively complex and able to master contradictions.

We have also learnt, however, that creativity can be achieved through following particular steps and through enhancing our repertoire of skills and knowledge. Intelligence is, to a certain extent, something that we are born with, but it can also be expanded throughout the life course.

Skills and intelligence must also be applied in order to produce creative results. Our intuition, or unconscious, plays an important part in this process. However, a combination of processes must come together in the creative process that include:

- immersion in information and appropriate selection

SUNDAY

MONDAY

TUESDAY

WEDNESDAY

THURSDAY

FRIDAY

SATURDAY

- the combination and connection of ideas and concepts, often unconsciously
- evaluating insights.

We can improve our chances of being able to produce creative results by ensuring that we get enough sleep and time for relaxation. We can also try to create the right environment to encourage and foster creative thinking: productive thought may not necessarily take place in a conventional environment, such as the workplace; it is more likely to occur in a natural and relaxed atmosphere.

Fact-check (answers at the back)

1. Which of the following statements is true?
   a) Creative people are more intelligent than the general population. ❑
   b) Being intelligent guarantees that a person will be creative. ❑
   c) Being creative has nothing to do with being intelligent. ❑
   d) Creative people are not usually any more intelligent than the general population. ❑

2. Creative people are naturally:
   a) extroverts ❑
   b) introverts ❑
   c) very competitive ❑
   d) without a particular personality trait ❑

3. Those considered to be creative tend to be:
   a) lacking in confidence ❑
   b) conventional ❑
   c) not very intelligent ❑
   d) determined to succeed ❑

4. Which of the following is not an aspect of intelligence?
   a) verbal ❑
   b) visuospatial ❑
   c) memory ❑
   d) bodily ❑

5. Which of the following should we do first in the creative process?
   a) collect/select all the relevant information ❑
   b) fit the pieces of the jigsaw together ❑
   c) verify the information ❑
   d) evaluate what we know ❑

6. Which of the following is incorrect? To be a creative thinker you will need:
   a) a willingness to generate ideas ❑
   b) only limited general knowledge ❑
   c) a large waste bin ❑
   d) a surplus of energy and attention ❑

7. Which of the following is not a useful strategy for improving creativity?
   a) accessing your unconscious ❑
   b) reinstating your intuition ❑
   c) developing a sense of curiosity – asking challenging questions ❑
   d) focusing on things that you do not normally enjoy ❑

8. Where/when are you least likely to come up with a creative idea?
a) when listening to music ❑
b) when in the workplace ❑
c) when travelling by bus/plane ❑
d) when 'dreaming and drifting' ❑

9. A good night's sleep can make you:
a) 10 per cent smarter ❑
b) 20 per cent smarter ❑
c) 40 per cent smarter ❑
d) 60 per cent smarter ❑

10. The right amount of sleep has:
a) a positive effect on creativity ❑
b) no effect on creativity ❑
c) a negative effect on creativity ❑
d) no relation at all to the functioning of the brain ❑

SUNDAY

MONDAY

TUESDAY

WEDNESDAY

THURSDAY

FRIDAY

SATURDAY

THURSDAY

Creative problem-solving

*Reason can answer questions, but
imagination has to ask them.*

Ralph N Gerard

Today we will look at applying creativity to tackle real-world problems.

Have you ever been stuck on a problem and found it useful to step back and return to it later from an entirely different direction? You may even have come across a better solution. This is called lateral thinking, and we shall learn how this sort of creative thinking technique can be extremely useful for many scenarios.

We will also see how creativity can be used to help solve large-scale systems problems more typical of those found in organizations, where problems are not always simple and bounded.

You probably know already that not everyone solves a problem in exactly the same way. We shall look at the processes and different types of thinking involved in problem-solving and also some of the preferences and roles that individuals can take on. As you read, think about how you solve problems – what role do you take if you are in a group and what thought processes do you go through? Could you employ more creativity to your problem-solving? Today we will find out how.

Applying creativity

There is a strong body of research, based on empirical study of how people tackle real problems, that has developed into a description of the sequence by which substantial problems are tackled. This describes a general framework or a model of the overall process that encompasses all of the subprocesses that need to be involved. It is based on the work of Osborn (the inventor of brainstorming) in the 1950s, which was developed by Sidney Parnes and further refined by Isakson and Treffinger, whose approach we use here. Research identified about six separate sub-processes involved in successfully solving problems. These are collected into three main stages:

1 understanding the problem
2 generating ideas
3 planning for action.

At any of these stages, both divergent and convergent thinking processes are involved.

Divergent thinking

This means thinking outwards or widening the options. Successful divergent thinking involves:

● fluency – generating a large number of responses
● flexibility – increasing the scope or the range of different ideas generated
● originality – including the unlikely or unusual aspects of ideas.

Convergent thinking

This means narrowing down the options or selecting specific ideas. It is used to analyse, develop, refine and otherwise evaluate options.

It has sometimes, wrongly, been assumed that creativity is all about divergent thinking. This is a mistake, as rounded and robust creative and problem-solving behaviour is always balanced by the more evaluative and convergent thinking.

The richest and most complete description of the CPS (creative problem-solving) process is shown in the diagram below.

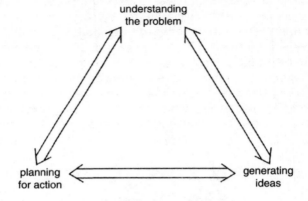

As the diagram above implies, these three primary stages are mutually interdependent. Individual problem-solvers and individual problems may require not only starting at any point, but also moving backwards and forwards through the whole process. The table below does not imply that there are six sequential stages. What it does imply, though, is that robust problem-solving will – mostly – involve activity at all stages.

	Divergent thinking	Convergent thinking
Understanding the problem		
Mess finding	Seeking opportunities for problem-solving	Establishing a broad general goal
Data finding	Examining detail from multiple perspectives	Identifying the most important data
Problem finding	Many possible problem statements	Selecting specific problem statements
Generating ideas		
Idea finding	Producing many ideas	Identifying rich options
Planning for action		
Solution finding	Developing criteria for evaluation of options	Choosing and applying criteria
Acceptance finding	Evaluating possible actions	Formulating a plan of action

If you can think of an example of flawed problem-solving or decision-making in your own organization you will probably be able to identify from the model the weak or missing stage that contributed to the difficulty.

However, it can sometimes even be an advantage to subvert the process and come at a problem from a totally different direction. This usually happens when any of the underlying assumptions of a problem are subverted or challenged. Edward de Bono calls this type of thinking lateral thinking.

Murray Gell-Mann, in his fascinating book *The Quark and the Jaguar*, recounts a story of lateral thinking.

Case study

How can you use a barometer to measure the height of a building? This exam question does have one 'real' answer that the examiner was, no doubt, expecting. However, the student's response was to tie the barometer to a piece of string, drop it from the building and then measure its length. When challenged, various other solutions were offered. One involved offering the janitor of the building a 'prize' of a barometer if he would tell the student the height of the building.

Systems thinking

Specialized problem-solving approaches have been developed
to tackle particular types or classes of problem. Kepner and
Tregoe developed an algorithm to deal with 'deviation from
the norm'-type problems. They use an interesting approach to
describing problem situations using:

- identity
- location
- time
- magnitude

as dimensions in describing the problems.

More recently, a set of approaches has been developed to
tackle open systems- or soft systems-type problems. These
are situations that are characterized by:

- uncertainty
- ambiguity
- dynamic relationships between components of the system
- feedback from the external environment into the system.

The creative part here is often in the analysis phase of our
generalized CPS process. It is required to analyse the systemic
structure of the dynamic system. Typical system problems
might include:

- stock level fluctuation in supply chains
- supply and demand problems
- the effect of work volumes on quality.

They can be tackled by drawing system diagrams that show the
dynamic relationships between the components and variables
of the system. They can then be modelled using specialized
computer software.

These large-scale systems problems that organizations have
to tackle require the development of an enhanced repertoire of
analytical and creative thinking skills. These include the ability to:

- seek behind surface data
- obtain data in creative ways
- map relationships between variables

- identify patterns and regularity in situations
- understand cause and effect processes
- draw inferences and conclusions
- map and model systems.

Problem-finding

We have emphasized above that each problem and situation brings with it different requirements. This means that, in practice, we will approach different problems in individual ways, but there is an implicit suggestion that there are different kinds of problems.

Can we classify or characterize these different kinds of problems? The answer, of course, is yes. And it is important to do so, for two reasons. First, different kinds of problems place different kinds of requirements on us. Second, and more importantly, as individuals we will seek out those kinds of problems that suit our interests, preferences and circumstances.

But where do problems come from? Of course, they can come from almost any source, but some typical sources are:

- The external environment: forces outside our own organization or unit can create confrontational situations or the pressure to change.
- The internal environment: the need to fix, enhance, improve or update products, services or systems.
- Our own psychology: our own preferences and style of doing things, together with our need to manage or control, can create a need to do things differently, or to do different things.

It is a mistake, however, to think that problems come to our attention via a single route. Some problems are there in front of our eyes and can hardly be ignored. Yet others emerge as we immerse ourselves deeper into our chosen domain. There are yet others that we create by virtue of our own interests and perspectives on our working context. For other people they may not be problems at all. They arrive not by simple recognition, but by us actively seeking new interpretations of current data or by inventing entirely new ways of looking at the world. These give us different types of problem:

● Presented problems: these are evident in the system, and are recognized by all on the basis of data currently in the system.
● Discovered problems: these are implicitly embedded in current data, but need to be discovered by 'digging out' or otherwise probing.
● Constructed problems: these are the problems that have the potential to exist, but have to be actively created or invented.

When was the last time you encountered a genuine constructed problem? Try inventing such a problem for your own working environment.

By implication, there is an increase in the creative input required to find and tackle these different classes of problems, as we go down the list. The problems are also more difficult to articulate progressively further along the continuum from presented through to constructed problems. The latter are the territory of the genuine visionary in a given context or domain.

Case study

In the early 1990s someone had the idea of pre-chopping, washing and packaging lettuce. This was just a bright idea for which there was no historical market. This was a solution for which no problem existed. In 1999 the US market for packaged lettuce was worth $1.1 billion.

If it is possible to do this with a head of lettuce, what's your excuse?

Gary Hamel

Personal style

We have implied that there are significant differences in the way that individuals apply themselves to creative problem-solving in real-life situations. In relation to the CPS, some people adopt a linear, orderly progression through the stages. Alternatively, some take a more non-linear complex and random walk through those stages. Added to this, we, clearly, as individuals have our own strengths and weaknesses in relation to different stages of the total process.

Personal preferences and types

One way to get a 'fix' on some of these individual differences is to look at a framework for describing them. One of the most used and most useful frameworks is the Myers–Briggs type indicator. This was based on the work of the Swiss psychologist CG Jung, who observed clear differences in the ways people approached the world, and thus developed his typology. Based on his ideas, the Myers–Briggs type indicator measures four key scales of differences or preference in individuals.

They are:

- Extroversion (E) vs. introversion (I): this is to do with whether we draw energy from external stimuli (E) or the inner world of thoughts (I).
- Sensing (S) vs. intuition (N): this is the scale of perception. Do we pay attention to hard, concrete facts and details (S) or to pattern, overview or the bigger picture of ideas (N)?

- Thinking (T) vs. feeling (F): this is the decision-making scale. Are we logical, objective and scientific (T) or do we base decisions on more people-centred criteria or values (F)?
- Judging (J) vs. perceiving (P): this reflects our approach to the world. Is it ordered, controlled, sequential (J) or flexible and spontaneous (P)?

Our preferences on these scales will influence our preferences and strengths in relation to problem-solving. In fact, we can draw up the stages of a problem-solving process in respect of the scales.

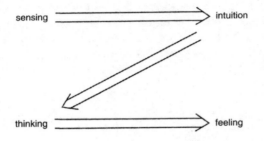

The stages involve:

- Sensing – collecting basic facts and figures and hard data.
- Intuition – drawing the facts together, making connections and identifying patterns.
- Thinking – rational and ordered decision-making.
- Feeling – evaluating options and decisions for consequences and effects on others.

Our preferences on the J-scale might tell us a great deal about how we approach the total process.

Roles in problem-solving

There have been many attempts to classify and describe the types of strength, style and contribution of different individuals in group and co-operative problem-solving situations. The Belbin team roles profile is one example. The weakness of this for our purposes is that there is an implication that creativity is confined to or concentrated in a minority of the roles.

There are a number of classifications that look at roles specifically in relation to creativity. Edward de Bono's idea of the six thinking hats is well known and widely used.

The hats involve participants in a type of mental role-play:

- white hat – an objective look at data and information
- red hat – feelings, hunches, intuition
- black hat – logical negative, caution, being judgemental
- yellow hat – logical positive, feasibility and benefits
- green hat – new ideas, creative thinking
- blue hat – control of process.

The value of such a framework is that it is simple and it encompasses a good range of creative problem-solving sub-processes, with a balance of convergent and divergent thought. The disadvantages are that it might be difficult to remember which hat is which, and that it can be perceived as artificial.

Summary

Today's chapter has described the tried and trusted framework for creative problem-solving, with its three principal stages: understanding the problem, generating ideas and planning for action. Next time you stumble across a problem, try solving it with this framework in mind. Remember that the stages are interdependent but you won't necessarily move through them linearly.

We have also learned about the different types of thinking required for problem solving, the benefits of each and how to apply them. We focused on divergent (widening the options) and convergent thinking (narrowing the options).

In addition, we have looked at different kinds of problems and how we arrive at problems in a real-life working environment. Sometimes the best solutions are found when the problem isn't even known! This is the most creative way of solving problems, and we call it problem finding.

SUNDAY

MONDAY

TUESDAY

WEDNESDAY

THURSDAY

FRIDAY

SATURDAY

We have also considered personal differences and approaches to problem solving, to allow you to understand your own strengths, weaknesses and personal style. Frameworks for this include the Myers–Brigg type indicator, Belbin's team roles and Edward de Bono's six coloured thinking hats.

Fact-check (answers at the back)

1. In organizations, creativity is best:
   a) as a co-operative activity applied to real-world situations ❑
   b) as an activity practised alone ❑
   c) when practised only by managers ❑
   d) when it is not called upon ❑

2. There are three main stages to problem-solving. Which one is incorrect?
   a) understanding the problem ❑
   b) ticking boxes ❑
   c) planning for action ❑
   d) generating ideas ❑

3. Divergent thinking means:
   a) thinking outwards or widening the options ❑
   b) looking at a mirror ❑
   c) reducing the number of options ❑
   d) not solving the problem ❑

4. Successful divergent thinking involves:
   a) being restrictive ❑
   b) thinking of only one solution ❑
   c) repeating the question ❑
   d) flexibility ❑

5. Convergent thinking:
   a) should not be used in problem-solving ❑
   b) means widening the options ❑
   c) is used to analyse, develop, refine and evaluate options ❑
   d) should not complement divergent thinking in problem-solving ❑

6. Problem-solving will not involve:
   a) a strict sequential movement through the six stages ❑
   b) seeking opportunities ❑
   c) generating ideas ❑
   d) finding a mess ❑

7. Lateral thinking involves:
   a) coming at a problem from a different direction ❑
   b) not challenging any underlying assumptions to the problem ❑
   c) using a barometer ❑
   d) asking someone else to solve the problem for you ❑

8. Constructed problems...
   a) have the potential to exist but have to be actively created or invented ❑
   b) require the least amount of creative input to solve ❑
   c) are easy to articulate ❑
   d) are recognized by all ❑

9. Which statement is correct?
   a) Every person solves a problem in the same way. ❑
   b) Every person adopts a linear, orderly progression through the problem-solving stages. ❑
   c) Every person has the same strengths in solving problems. ❑
   d) There are significant differences in the way that individuals apply themselves to problem-solving. ❑

10. A framework used to describe individual ways of solving problems is the:
   a) Myers–Brigg type indicator ❑
   b) Richter indicator ❑
   c) Saffir–Simpson indicator ❑
   d) Beaufort indicator ❑

SUNDAY

MONDAY

TUESDAY

WEDNESDAY

THURSDAY

FRIDAY

SATURDAY

Tools and techniques

> *The active process leading to creativity is metaphorical in nature.*
>
> Don Faben

It might now be useful to think of creativity as a skill – something that is not just innate, but which can be learned and developed. Today we shall be looking at the range of methods that are available to help you enhance your creativity.

Idea generation, or ideation, is central to most of the techniques on which we will be focusing. But we will also cover a number of approaches that are slightly more convergent and analytical.

How often have you found it easier to describe something using an image or analogy? The different approaches we will encounter in this chapter involve some combination of, or focus on, the verbal, visual and metaphorical. In fact, you are probably already employing creative techniques like these every day without even realizing it. Brainstorming, for example, is probably the most widely known creativity-enhancing technique, and we will look at it in some detail – the theory behind it, its usefulness for groups and individuals and how best to use it.

To round off today's chapter we take a brief look at some other intriguing techniques, namely synectics, attribute zapping and chindogu. We see how, with a bit of creative thinking, chocolate, bricks and airline food can all have something in common...

Ideation

Most of the techniques that are around are designed to enhance the production of idea generation. This is because, on the whole, the evaluation components of the creative continuum are to some extent easier and more natural activities. Perhaps this is because they are more 'left brained'. It is also because people view the ideation stage as being inherently:

● more creative
● more difficult
● less culturally acceptable or 'natural'
● more valuable.

The nature of tools and techniques

Although we shall also concentrate on the tools and techniques for idea generation, we shall cover a number of approaches that are more convergent and analytical.

We should note that in relation to these tools and techniques, a number of useful distinctions should be made. The first one is between groups and individuals. Some of these ideas are very much group focused. They are based on the notion that working in groups adds synergy to idea generation. That is, the sum of the parts is more than the whole.

Synergy

2 + 2 = 5

One of the underlying assumptions is that creative activity is accumulative amongst a group of individuals, so that a group will produce more or better ideas than if the individuals were to work alone. However, most, if not all, of these techniques can be used individually.

It is interesting to note that creative techniques involve engaging different aspects of our thought processes. Of course, individual differences mean that we use unique combinations of different kinds of processes, but it is also true that different people favour some over others.

On the whole, the different approaches involve some combination of or focus on the verbal, visual and metaphorical.

Verbal

A great deal of our thought processes are based around language. There is a close relationship between concepts and language. Therefore, it makes sense for many people to use verbal techniques to provoke or elicit ideas.

Give your brain a workout by trying to guess what these well-known phrases or sayings represent:

1 KJUSTK
2 YOUJUSTME
3 GET IT GET IT GET IT GET IT
4 ie.
5 INVA DERS

You have to dig quite deep for the answers to these, don't you? Did you notice that most of your processing happened under the level of consciousness? The lateral and associative talents of your brain need to be applied, as it is very difficult to arrive at the answers by purely logical, sequential means.

Visual

A picture is worth a thousand words

Most of us live in complex and overloaded information spaces. On a daily basis we can quite easily reach the limit of our brain's ability to consciously process and retain information in a useful form. It is not surprising that we need to develop tools and techniques that help us to cope with this overload. There is a lot of assistance and technology available to enable us to process information once it is organized and externalized. But there is much less help when it comes to the primary information processor available – the brain.

For many people the visual channel is the primary means of dealing with complex, conceptual information. Dealing with large amounts of information and the relationships between the components of the information can only be done visually by many.

Concept space maps (or microcosms) are a rich tool for displaying such information. They are visual arrangements that show concepts 'in relation to'. They encapsulate large amounts of complex data in a 'mind's eye chunk'.

Thus, they mirror the natural associative and relational patterns of the brain. Using the power of your visual imagination, microcosm diagrams will help you visualize concepts in this relational way.

We will set out some of the archetypal forms and schemas with which the brain can map conceptual spaces. It takes a little time to learn how to use them because, for some, practice is necessary. However, the benefits are enormous.

The basic format is a simple spider diagram (sometimes called a mindmap), with a natural, associative structure.

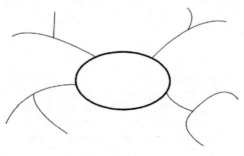

The lines can represent relationships such as:

- breaks down into (hierarchy)
- is a consequence of (cause and effect)
- follows (sequence)
- implies (logical connectivity)
- is related to.

However, it is easy to add structure and order to these in some of the following ways.

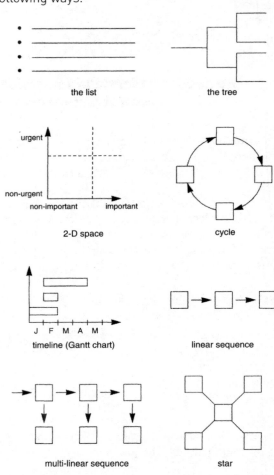

the list

the tree

2-D space

cycle

timeline (Gantt chart)

linear sequence

multi-linear sequence

star

These can be used for recalling, crystallizing, organizing, summarizing or synthesizing ideas. They have proved extremely useful in many of the following applications:

- note-taking
- problem-solving
- cognitive mapping (sharing mental models)
- report-planning and writing
- presentations
- process-mapping
- algorithms.

Metaphorical

We need to understand something of the causal structure of the world.
Steven Pinker

Because the modern world has grown away from our primitive intuitions about it, we have to invent devices to help us understand it. Analogies and metaphors are powerful ways of doing this.

You do not have to look far in the worlds of science, the arts, culture or society to see how widely we use metaphor and analogy to encapsulate our world. The worlds of management, business and organizations also use metaphor as a means of articulating and communicating identity and purpose.

You may have spotted some of the following things being used as metaphors yourself:

- health
- food
- machines/mechanical
- branching tree
- computing/the internet
- chaos theory.

Of course, you can also invent your own. They can be very useful for provoking and eliciting ideas.

Case study

I did some training in an organization that was trying to communicate the importance of customer focus, teamwork, financial results and safety. Because safety was in danger of becoming the 'poor relation' of the four, management used the analogy of juggling the fourth ball – it was difficult but the trick had to be pulled off. The analogy proved a potent tool. Even the chairman, addressing a management forum, mimed a juggle as he spoke about the importance of safety.

Major changes and breakthroughs usually involve a change in the metaphorical backdrop. In fact, by engineering such changes we can achieve the sort of paradigm shift in perspective associated with major change in organizations.

The visual, verbal and metaphorical modes can be used in all of the techniques that follow.

Brainstorming

First and foremost among creative techniques is the idea of brainstorming. It is the one technique that almost everybody knows. It was developed by Alex Osborn in the 1950s, and it focuses on the elicitation of ideas. Its main aim is to generate more and better ideas. The key belief is that we tend to evaluate ideas too early in the formation of creative solutions. Thus, we have a habit of killing good ideas at their source. This also creates in people an apprehension or a disinclination to go public with their ideas for fear of overly critical comments that reflect on the individual. This has the effect of inhibiting the declaration and flow of new ideas.

Thus, the classic approach to brainstorming involves two underpinning ideas. First, ideas are created and recorded without judgement at the initial stage. Any idea is as good as any other. That is, we separate the production from the evaluation. They are separate processes, and their interrelationship is not neutral as evaluation can inhibit production. This separation is the key benefit of the idea of brainstorming as a tool. Second, the more ideas, the better.

Quantity breeds quality. Brainstorming groups operate a set of conventions:

- criticism is ruled out
- freewheeling is welcome
- quantity is good
- combine and improve where you can.

Only when sufficient ideas have been generated can they be evaluated. There are a number of ways that this can be arranged. For instance, a smaller subset of people or a separate set of people can evaluate. Alternatively, criteria for evaluation can be set and agreed prior to the brainstorming session.

There have been some very strong claims for the benefits of brainstorming as a technique. However, it is not a panacea, and the evidence is equivocal on whether groups produce more or better ideas than a collection of individuals.

The use of brainstorming has been studied by Professors Adrian Furnham and Barrie Gunter. They found that groups performing well-structured tasks tend to make better, more accurate decisions. However, they take more time to reach decisions than individuals would. In poorly structured tasks individuals perform better than groups. They are more productive and work faster. It would seem, then, that groups are less efficient than individuals at generating ideas.

However, I think that the value of brainstorming may lie in a different direction. It could be that it provides structure to an activity that is not often legitimated in many organizations – the free rein of ideas, however silly or apparently inappropriate. It provides a framework and it legitimates explicit creative behaviour. It also has a sociological dimension in that it is a way of sharing ideas, sharing meanings and sharing the outcomes.

One way to improve the productivity of brainstorming groups is to provide a real mix of people, and their skills, approaches and backgrounds. This adds to the 'spark' and widens the scope of potential ideas.

Other useful techniques

Synectics

Originated by William Gordon, synectics is the joining together of unassociated irrelevant elements. It picks up on the notion that analogy is a natural creative activity. Many accounts of how natural creatives and geniuses go about their work seem to reveal that analogy often comes into it. There are two parts:

1 When dealing with a problem, make a connection between the unfamiliar and the familiar. This is called making the strange familiar. This can be done by asking questions like 'How is a leaf like a snack?' (Answer: If it's a Pringle.)
2 There is a need to look at the problem from a variety of different perspectives – the search for novel viewpoints. This is called making the familiar strange. Ask questions like 'How is a chocolate bar like an animal?' (Answer: It's a Lion.)

To help elicit ideas you can 'chunk up' and 'chunk down' logical categories by generalizing or specifying. So, a crisp becomes a snack, which becomes food, and so on.

Attribute zapping

One of the archetypal tests for creativity activities is to find a use for a familiar object. For instance, in the creativity column by William Hartson in the *Independent*, readers were asked to do just that.

- Q. What can you do with an odd sock?
    - Use as a tool to measure right ankles
    - Set up emotional reunion with another sock on TV
    - Protect cucumbers from frost
    - TV show – one foot in the sock
    - Cushion for a pogo stick
    - Feed it baked beans and use it as a wind sock
    - Starch it and use it as a boomerang
    - Leave it hanging around bars in the hope of picking up some fluff
    - Penpal for Bill Clinton's cat
    - 'How can a single sock go walkabout?'

Can you find any others? Try a simpler one:

- Q. How many uses can you find for a brick?

A way to think up uses would be to look at the attributes of the brick and generate ideas from each one of these. So, for instance, we can describe a brick as:

- red
- rough
- cuboid
- sharp-edged
- heavy
- having two holes.

To create uses for a brick just take each attribute in turn and ask, for example, 'What can I do with the sharp edges?', 'What can I do with the redness?', and so on.

Chindogu

So how do we begin to turn ideas into products?

Chindogu is a lovely transitional idea. It is a Japanese notion that comes from the word 'chin' meaning unusual, and 'dogu' meaning tool. It is a gadget that appears to be useful but really isn't. The rules for a chindogu are that they must be capable of being made, but must not be useful (just nearly useful). It is gratuitous invention, with the main purpose being fun. Here are some rules:

- It must make our life more convenient in some way but must also make it inconvenient in another way.
- It can't be for real use.
- It must actually work.
- It has a spirit of anarchy.
- It is a tool for everyday life.
- It is humorous in some way.

Examples are:

- Swiss army glove – a glove with a tool on each digit
- hay fever dispenser – a toilet roll holder that sits on the head to dispense toilet roll for hay fever sufferers.

These were some of my favourites, and were invented at a creativity and innovation workshop in Romania.

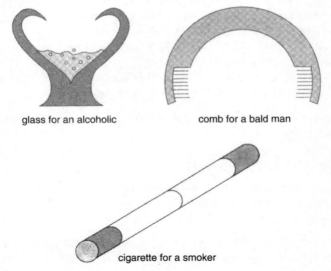

glass for an alcoholic   comb for a bald man

cigarette for a smoker

The nine-year-old son of a participant in that workshop, concerned about my smoking, invented and offered me this chindogu cigarette! As we now have such a thing as a commercial comforter cigarette, this one might fail on being too useful. It does, however, show the value of chindogu as a transitional device for getting from gratuitous invention to nearer to product.

These inventions, no matter how daft they seem, can then be evaluated. Can we see any sense in them? Could they be the spark for any really useful ideas? Because the starting point for chindogus are the little irritations of normal life, and they happen in the stimuli of everyday contexts and settings, it would be quite possible to use real settings, situations or irritations to begin the process.

For instance, move on from chindogus to look at airline food. We all know it is a problem. But how can we go about inventing a better version? We can do it by listing every aspect of airline food, and questioning, challenging, reversing and reinventing each in turn. We are effectively finding out what 'knobs' our concept of airline food has, and modulating each one in turn. In that way it is quite like attribute zapping.

- Attribute – you eat on the plane.
  - Why? Is it possible to eat before take-off?
- Attribute – everybody eats at the same time.
  - Why? What would it look like if we didn't? Self-service?
- Attribute – it is delivered on a tray.
  - Why? Can it be delivered another way? Drinks through a pipe with a personal tap at the seat, perhaps?

In this way, you can take real situations and use them to develop product ideas.

Specific techniques

Certain tools and techniques have been developed to suit specific circumstances. Some that might be useful for further reading include:

- force field diagrams – for analysing driving and restraining forces in change situations

- Ishikawa (fishbone) diagrams – for problem-solving
- SWOT analysis – for identifying and evaluating internal factors (strengths and weaknesses) and external factors (opportunities and threats) in organizational contexts.

Summary

Today we have set out some of the key tools and techniques that can assist you in developing creative ideas. It would be impossible to cover all of the many techniques that have been developed, and not everybody will respond to all that have been presented, but you should find a few that suit your own style of working. We have considered techniques in the three primary modes of working: the verbal, visual and metaphorical. Experiment and find what technique works best for you – you are perhaps even already using it subconsciously.

Brainstorming is the most common and well-known technique. But some people misunderstand it. For it to be successful two ideas need to be borne in mind. One, that ideas are created and recorded without judgement at the initial stage – every idea should be treated equally. Two, the more ideas the better – quantity breeds quality. Only when these tactics are employed will brainstorming be truly effective.

SUNDAY
MONDAY
TUESDAY
WEDNESDAY
THURSDAY
FRIDAY
SATURDAY

We have also looked at some other useful interesting techniques: synectics, attribute zapping and chindogu. At first, they may seem strange, but they have probably got your brain thinking on different levels – and that is what creativity is all about.

Fact-check (answers at the back)

1. Most techniques for enhancing creativity are designed to enhance:
   a) appearance ❏
   b) your CV ❏
   c) status ❏
   d) idea generation ❏

2. The ideation stage is considered:
   a) more creative, more difficult and more valuable ❏
   b) the easiest stage ❏
   c) the quickest to complete ❏
   d) the least valuable ❏

3. Working in groups . . .
   a) adds synergy to idea generation ❏
   b) is time-consuming and unhelpful ❏
   c) increases the chances of conflict ❏
   d) is noisy and worthless ❏

4. A picture is worth . . .
   a) less than a digital photo ❏
   b) a thousand words ❏
   c) the same as the description ❏
   d) usually around £500 ❏

5. Approaches to creativity-enhancing techniques do not involve:
   a) verbal ❏
   b) foreign language ❏
   c) metaphorical ❏
   d) visual ❏

6. Choose the correct statement.
   a) Metaphors are a waste of time. ❏
   b) Metaphors and analogies should not be used to provoke ideas. ❏
   c) Many people can only deal with complex information visually. ❏
   d) Using verbal techniques will never elicit a response. ❏

7. Choose the correct statement.
   a) Using a mindmap creates further problems. ❏
   b) Mindmaps are never useful for preparing presentations. ❏
   c) Mindmaps result in even more confusion. ❏
   d) Lines in a mindmap can represent relationships such as hierarchy and cause and effect. ❏

8. Which statement is correct?
   a) Brainstorming inhibits new ideas. ❏
   b) When it comes to brainstorming, the fewer ideas the better. ❏
   c) In brainstorming, there is always one idea better than all of the others. ❏
   d) Brainstorming encourages the free reign of ideas. ❏

9. Three useful techniques for enhancing creativity are:
a) fly swatting, synthetics, sudoku ❏
b) brainwashing, chindogu, attribute zapping ❏
c) attribute zapping, synectics, chindogu ❏
d) sudoku, synthetics, chindogu ❏

10. Chindogu is a creativity-enhancing technique based on an idea from:
a) Japan ❏
b) Germany ❏
c) Peru ❏
d) Canada ❏

SUNDAY

MONDAY

TUESDAY

WEDNESDAY

THURSDAY

FRIDAY

SATURDAY

SATURDAY

Creativity in organizations

*We don't know who first discovered water,
but we can be sure it wasn't a fish.*

Howard George

We have now come full circle – to talk about
organizations again. Having painted the strategic
context on Sunday, we will round off the week by
looking at some key themes and considerations that
organizations should be heeding. We move from
describing the what of the situations and imperatives
involved to the how of the strategies for dealing
with them.

Creativity is crucial to an organization. It flows
through its every aspect – from its culture, its
systems and architecture, to its products and
services. Creativity is *required* for success.

We will take ourselves on the journey from idea
to product, or the creative continuum as it is often
known. This is a journey that is long and never linear,
with many hurdles along the way, but when it is
completed properly it can lead to great success. We
use the pharmaceutical industry as an example to
demonstrate the complicated steps that are involved.

It is often said that *knowledge is power*. Today we
shall see that there is a knowledge pipeline as much
as there is a product pipeline. How can we get the best
out of people in our organizations, to maximize brain
power? We will see today what sort of organizational
culture is needed to nurture creativity so it, and its
people, can reach its full potential.

The creative continuum

Creative behaviour at work can be difficult for any individual to accomplish. So when we generalize that outwards, to the operation of creativity in groups and teams, and on again from there to organizations, it becomes very complicated indeed. It is a question that touches every aspect of what an organization is – from its culture, through its systems and architecture, to its products and services.

WE'VE COME TO UNBLOCK THE CREATIVITY

Creativity (or the lack of it) is not a single problem that can be treated separately and fixed with ease. Creativity in organizations operates in more dynamic, subtle and complex ways.

For much of this book we have talked about ideation. But ideation in and of itself is not enough. There are many examples of great ideas that took inordinate efforts to become successful products. Examples include the tortuous process by which the wind-up radio became a product – with the help of Nelson Mandela. The Dyson bagless vacuum cleaner needed literally hundreds of prototypes to become the finished saleable article.

If even brilliant ideas like this take so much effort, just think how many millions of good ideas are lost along the way. Only an incredibly small proportion of ideas reach maturity and implementation. Even in organizations where there is a sufficiency of good ideas, there can be (and often are) major blockages and hurdles to the realization of those ideas.

From idea to product

We can conclude from this that there is a linked set of processes involved in the bringing of an idea to fulfilment. We can call this the creative continuum.

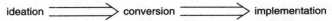

ideation ══════⟹ conversion ══════⟹ implementation

At the left-hand side we have ideation – the generation of ideas.

In the middle we have conversion – the intermediate stage where ideas are brought to fruition through design.

At the right-hand side we have implementation – where the new product/service is brought to market. It is only if we can move right through the creative continuum that we have genuine innovation.

To study a case, such as the development of the wind-up radio, gives some of the flavour of the persistence and effort (as well as the disappointment) involved in moving from left to right.

The stages are a collection of steps that include:

- a switch from divergent to convergent thinking
- the collection, organization and verification of information
- various aspects of ideation
- prototyping, model-building and refinement of ideas
- refinement, rejection and reinvention of ideas
- application of reality check, evaluation and validation.

Organizations can be 'mapped' using a diagram like the one below to illustrate their strengths and blockages.

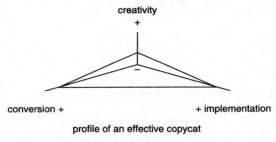

profile of an effective copycat

The continuum is a generalized description. Some sectors have their own quite detailed versions of the same thing. This is particularly relevant for organizations that are heavily involved in research and development or rely heavily on a stream of new products for survival.

The product pipeline

In many industries and organizations these steps are quite formalized and structured. Take the pharmaceutical industry as an example. They call the steps from the creation of a compound to the marketing of a finished compliant product 'the pipeline'. The extreme ends of this pipeline are characterized as far from market and near to market.

It involves a series of complicated steps including:

- discovery of compounds
- development of drug substance
- development of clinical form
- development of market form
- pre-clinical research
- clinical research
- biostats
- regulatory.

Most organizations are not as structured. However, it is worthwhile looking at the notion of a pipeline. It is normally easy to guess where ideas get killed in most organizations, and it is often early on.

Organizational culture and innovation

> *The single greatest challenge facing managers in the developed world is to raise the productivity of knowledge and service workers. This challenge ... will ultimately determine the competitive performance of companies.*
>
> Peter Drucker

Organizations need to know how well they are doing. If creativity and innovation are important, they need to understand their own strengths and weaknesses. How can they go about doing this?

Auditing creativity

The pipeline is an interesting idea that can help to measure or evaluate effectiveness and efficiency at various stages of the creative continuum. The focus for attention shifts throughout the different stages.

At the left-hand side, the primary focus should be on the organizational environment – behaviour and the enabling culture.

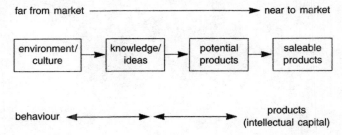

far from market ⟶ near to market

environment/culture → knowledge/ideas → potential products → saleable products

behaviour ⟷ ⟷ products (intellectual capital)

Typical categories to pay attention to here would include:

- effective team-working and collaboration
- professional development
- morale and motivation
- work and management style.

As we move to the right, we become more concerned with outcomes and products – so-called intellectual capital.

Knowledge management

We are just beginning to understand the massive power of knowledge, but we are at the very early stages of developing tools and processes to manage it properly.

There is a consensus that intellectual capital is what knowledge and service workers produce.

There is a 'knowledge pipeline' just as there is a product pipeline. It involves some of the following steps:

- acquisition or generation of information
- transformation of that information into knowledge
- storing and sharing of knowledge
- use of knowledge for innovation.

Case study

A recent research report on the subject of knowledge management was conducted by the consultancy KPMG. They noted from their survey of organizations that the majority have some kind of knowledge management programme, and there is wide appreciation of the need and the benefits of such programmes. However, they also point out that many fail to understand the full implications or to achieve the potential benefits.

Organizations are going to need to get much better at understanding, managing and enhancing these processes in order to compete for the future. If the message is 'maximize brainpower', then these are the ways in which the organization can genuinely become a learning organization.

So where do organizations stand in terms of investment and attention to basic research and development? There are a few clues in the following case study.

Case study

The Department of Trade and Industry annual research and development (R&D) scorecard shows Britain at the bottom of the spending league of industrial nations.

The largest spenders committed 4.4 per cent of turnover to R&D, while British companies spent only 2.3 per cent in 1996.

Although R&D was perceived as good, design was seen as a luxury or a cost.

This is despite the fact that extra spending on design produces a beneficial increase in turnover and profit.

That is, design has an impact on growth. A small increase in design can give a threefold return. Design-intensive industries tend to grow more rapidly.

Source: Survey of design activity in British industry for the Design Council, conducted by Centre for Economic Forecasting at London Business School.

How do management choose among the many new ideas competing for attention? How can the ideas get to be developed? Here are some important considerations:

- Does the management have detailed and comprehensive data?
- Are the data well organized?
- Does the organization encourage research?
- Does it encourage new ideas?
- Does it disseminate knowledge?
- Is it easy to try things out?

Enabling culture

We have already made the point that culture is an important component of providing the conditions for creativity to flourish within an organization. But what are the behaviours that enable knowledge to be shared and organizations to learn?

Arie de Geus is a retired executive of Shell. He wondered how blue tits managed to discover how to get through milk bottle tops better than robins, especially when, surprisingly, any individual robin was just as likely to discover the trick as any blue tit. The answer is because blue tits flock together, and thus communicate the discovery to others, whereas robins are territorial, and if they discovered the trick they kept it to themselves. We can conclude from this that flocking behaviour promotes knowledge and learning throughout communities. The lesson for organizations is obvious.

Strategies for nurturing creativity

It should be a key priority of management to ensure that creativity is developed and encouraged within the organization. Creativity is all about individuals. We need to make sure that we have the right people with the right skills. How can this be achieved?

The strategies can be summarized as follows:

1 Buy them: select the right people using the most up-to-date assessment processes, including psychometric testing ideas.
2 Assess and measure what you have got: buy or invent tools and methods for auditing what is important – from culture to intellectual property.
3 Grow them: train people in the importance of creativity and innovation, in the techniques for ideation, in how to develop ideas into products and in working co-operatively.
4 Develop management structures and processes: these need to enable, encourage and reward positive behaviour.
5 Change culture: this is the most important of all.

A substantial body of research on both sides of the Atlantic, and championed in the UK by the CIPD, has shown that issues of engagement and job satisfaction are the strongest influences on the performance of organizations. Part of the reson is that motivated staff are more creative. Good human resource practices had a greater influence on profitability than quality, technology and research and development.

The three key features indicating success were:

- the development of skills
- the development of a positive attitude among staff
- an empowering culture (autonomy, flexibility, ability to solve problems).

These are sobering thoughts, but if we are serious about innovation, the conclusion from all of this evidence is that organizations must shift their emphasis to the management of knowledge, to learning and to the culture that supports both.

Summary

You should now be thinking not about your own creativity but about that of your organization. What is your role in encouraging creativity in your organization? One of management's key priorities should be to ensure that creativity is developed and encouraged within their organization, and we have seen that culture is imperative to this.

Ideation in itself is not enough. To have a truly innovative product or outcome involves going through the creative continuum from start to end – from ideation through conversion to implementation. We used the pharmaceutical industry as an example of using a product pipeline, a formalized and structured creative continuum. However, unfortunately most organizations do not have this sort of formal structure in place and ideas often get killed early on.

Knowledge management is crucial to an organization's survival. What is your organization's approach to creativity? Does it have an enabling culture that nurtures creativity? Do people share their ideas or keep them to themselves? Think about the recommendations you could make to change or improve creativity in your organization.

SUNDAY
MONDAY
TUESDAY
WEDNESDAY
THURSDAY
FRIDAY
SATURDAY

Fact-check (answers at the back)

1. Choose the correct statement.
   a) Even in organizations where there are many good ideas, there are hurdles to the realization of those ideas. ❏
   b) Lack of creativity in an organization is a one-off problem that can be treated easily. ❏
   c) Every great idea becomes a successful product. ❏
   d) The Dyson cleaner required only one prototype before the final product. ❏

2. The creative continuum:
   a) never involves disappointment ❏
   b) moves from ideation through conversion to implementation ❏
   c) shows genuine innovation even if only a part is realized ❏
   d) is the same for every organization ❏

3. The product pipeline in the pharmaceutical industry:
   a) uses pipes to create new products ❏
   b) is always three weeks in duration ❏
   c) involves a number of complicated steps such as discovery of compounds ❏
   d) uses a unique smoking technique as its first step ❏

4. A knowledge pipeline:
   a) is exactly the same as a product pipeline ❏
   b) uses knowledge for innovation within organizations ❏
   c) stops the development of new products ❏
   d) gives power to the wrong people ❏

5. Intellectual capital is:
   a) Paris ❏
   b) not sought after by companies ❏
   c) useless ❏
   d) produced by knowledge and service workers ❏

6. For creativity, the organizational environment requires:
   a) effective team-working and collaboration ❏
   b) many tea breaks ❏
   c) more managers than staff ❏
   d) a shorter working day ❏

7. Knowledge management is:
   a) discouraged by managers ❏
   b) just another fad ❏
   c) measured in every organization ❏
   d) important to organizational survival ❏

8. One of management's key priorities should be to:
a) discourage co-operative working ❏
b) doodle all day to increase creativity ❏
c) ensure that creativity is developed and encouraged within the organization ❏
d) limit creativity among individuals ❏

9. Choose the correct statement.
a) Innovation requires the management of knowledge and learning. ❏
b) Positive attitude among staff is not important. ❏
c) Human resource practices have no impact on profitability. ❏
d) Financial performance is not dependent on job satisfaction. ❏

10. Successful organizations:
a) do not develop skills ❏
b) develop a positive attitude among staff ❏
c) prevent an empowering culture ❏
d) discourage training and development ❏

SUNDAY

MONDAY

TUESDAY

WEDNESDAY

THURSDAY

FRIDAY

SATURDAY

Surviving in tough times

Being creative isn't just a nice-to-have attribute: it is *indispensable* for success, both personally and in business, in our increasingly demanding environment. You can choose to regard creativity as unimportant if you wish, but if you do then be prepared to accept the often disagreeable consequences. The benefits of seeing creativity as crucial, however, will be that you see more and more situations with a new pair of eyes and as opportunities rather than problems. You've probably heard the expression *If you aren't part of the solution then you're part of the problem*. Being creative will help you be the former as opposed to the latter.

1 Meet new people

We have seen that creativity is 'wired in' to human nature. That means it is wired in to people you don't know at present and perhaps might not if you don't make an effort. Make it your business to meet new people and find out what it is that inspires them or makes them tick.

2 Do something new to relax

This may mean becoming a regular at an art gallery or reading books by new novelists. Listen to music that you haven't bothered with before. Get a dog. Teach it tricks. Get out of your comfort zone. Challenge yourself to have a new kind of fun.

3 Deal with failure positively

If what you are doing personally or in business doesn't work, then consider trying something completely different. Keeping on with the same approach might never work. It just might be time for something new, in which case you are responsible for creating whatever that is.

4 Waste time

You can't see the wood for the trees? Don't know where to begin? Can't see you way out of a mistake? Then take some time off, no matter how busy you are. Go for a walk. Have a cup of coffee in a new café. Do something that has nothing to do with your problem. Chances are that something will happen to change your perspective.

5 Don't waste time

Being creative means being creative as often as possible. Don't waste even one opportunity to be innovative in your response to a new problem. Just because you were creative yesterday doesn't mean you can take a holiday today.

6 Write it down

The act of writing can clear your thoughts. You might know what you mean and why, but you may have to persuade friends or colleagues who don't understand. So, if you want to holiday in Madrid rather than Paris, or open an office in Copenhagen instead of Stockholm, explain why in 500 compelling words that will influence others.

7 Have a plan for being made redundant

There's a recession on, or there might be one around the corner. Create a clear plan of what you would prefer to do if you are unfortunate enough to find yourself without work. Now consider implementing it anyway. What's stopping you?

8 Immerse yourself in social media

It may seem daunting at first, but immerse yourself in the world of Facebook and Twitter. Not only will you help to increase your own visibility and profile, you'll also hone in on your interests, converse with new people you might never have found otherwise, and find out the trends, news and opinions within your industry. Inspiration will hit and the ideas will flow – and then you can even start writing your own blog post!

9 Become good at something new

If you play chess well then take up running. If you run daily then how are your plans for learning Spanish coming along? You get the idea. The challenges these new skills and experiences pose will result in new ways of thinking, which in turn will help create new solutions.

10 Love your enemy

Collaborate with someone you wouldn't normally work with or be friends with. He or she may epitomize a nightmare for you in terms of approach to life. *That doesn't matter.* Swap notes on how you would solve each other's problems. Radical differences can produce the creative spark you might not have ignited on your own.

Answers

Sunday: 1c; 2c; 3b; 4b; 5b; 6b; 7c; 8a; 9d; 10a.

Monday: 1b; 2a; 3a; 4c; 5a; 6b; 7a; 8c; 9d; 10c.

Tuesday: 1d; 2b; 3c; 4d; 5a; 6c; 7c; 8b; 9d; 10a.

Wednesday: 1a; 2d; 3d; 4c; 5a; 6b; 7d; 8b; 9c; 10a.

Thursday: 1a; 2b; 3a; 4d; 5c; 6a; 7a; 8a; 9d; 10a.

Friday: 1d; 2a; 3a; 4b; 5b; 6c; 7d; 8d; 9c; 10a.

Saturday: 1a; 2b; 3c; 4b; 5d; 6a; 7d; 8c; 9a; 10b.

ALSO AVAILABLE IN THE 'IN A WEEK' SERIES

BODY LANGUAGE FOR MANAGEMENT • BOOKKEEPING AND ACCOUNTING • CUSTOMER CARE • SPEED READING • DEALING WITH DIFFICULT PEOPLE • EMOTIONAL INTELLIGENCE • FINANCE FOR NON-FINANCIAL MANAGERS • INTRODUCING MANAGEMENT • MANAGING YOUR BOSS • MARKET RESEARCH • NEURO-LINGUISTIC PROGRAMMING • OUTSTANDING CREATIVITY • PLANNING YOUR CAREER • SUCCEEDING AT INTERVIEWS • SUCCESSFUL APPRAISALS • SUCCESSFUL ASSERTIVENESS • SUCCESSFUL BUSINESS PLANS • SUCCESSFUL CHANGE MANAGEMENT • SUCCESSFUL COACHING • SUCCESSFUL COPYWRITING • SUCCESSFUL CVS • SUCCESSFUL INTERVIEWING

For information about other titles in the series, please visit www.inaweek.co.uk

ALSO AVAILABLE IN THE 'IN A WEEK' SERIES

For information about other titles in the series, please visit www.inaweek.co.uk